LETTERS FROM JANICE

Correspondence from the Astral Plane

LETTERS FROM JANICE

Correspondence from the Astral Plane

Wayne Hatford

Uni★Sun
P.O. Box 25421
Kansas City, MO 64119

This book is manufactured in the United States of America. Cover art by Bradley Dehner and distribution by The Talman Company.

The Talman Company, Inc.
150 Fifth Avenue
New York, N.Y. 10011

ISBN # 0-912949-07-4
LCCN: 87-050116

LETTERS FROM JANICE
Correspondence from the Astral Plane
by Wayne Hatford

DEDICATION

A very special Thanks to *all* whose energies helped create this book and put it in the Light.

To Julie, Charles, Marcia, and Robert for their loving support.

AUTHOR'S PREFACE

What is automatic writing?

It is a process of connecting with Spirit via the use of etheric energy, which is everywhere. This energy can be used to establish a communication link with a given spirit entity. My approach to automatic writing involves invoking spiritual protection, envisioning white light above, around and below me, then going into a meditative state. With pen on paper, I wait. The pen starts to move of its own accord and greetings which identify the entity begin to flow. The etheric link is established and communication can proceed for a period of time. Questions and answers are exchanged. My technique is to verbalize questions rather than think them. The answers come as rapidly as the questions are posed, speeding along on the paper. I let myself be guided by spirit, never knowing what words will follow those already written.

How did automatic writing contact with Janice begin?

We had been friends since 1977. Upon my return from a European trip, I learned of her death. I mourned, feeling the loss of a dear friend. Then I felt total Love around me. Sensing her vibrations to be present, I decided to try automatic writing. Janice was there. At first, the words were few and scrawling, but the link was established and later grew stronger. Her first message had to do with Love and her desire to communicate about her new level of existence to others. She said: "Let the communication flow." It has, fueled by loving feelings, which are the glue that supports the Universe.

This book then, is a collection of automatic writings from Janice, presented in chronological order, with virtually no editing. Janice experiences the Astral and, as she opens and learns, her growth is mirrored in each session. Her purpose is to teach with Love. May the reader consider Janice's experiences and ideas, and accept or reject them, according to what is appropriate for him or her.

Who is/was Janice?

One who chose to deal with numerous physical ailments in the lifetime just past.

She was at the center of a diverse network of people, always being caring, supportive, and nurturing toward others, no matter what physical problems she confronted. She loved many and they loved her.

Janice touched people to the core with her astute and incisive observations on life. She advised in a judicious and concise way, always respecting their individual beliefs and choices. Her natural curiosity about people and their foibles was unquenchable. A writer, she had a gift with words and self-expression. Once again she is writing, sending "letters" about her experiences on the Astral Plane. Her stated purpose is to teach: "No death, only life, and all must know this: Only life is the fact of the Universe; nothing ceases, everything IS." Janice, I welcome you and send you Love.

Your friend, Wayne

Note: On the following pages, all italic questions and comments are mine; everything else is Janice.

4 December 1984

Can you identify yourself?

Janice.

What is your message?

Beauty, Love.

Can you confirm that you are really Janice?

Cat power! *(Janice dearly loved cats.)*

Spontaneous dictation:

See the spirit. Love the way of the spirit. Let the past die with Love. Let the communication flow. All about this level of existence. I elected to serve. Jeeves.

5 October 1985 (P.S.)

**Re: Jeeves:* There was personal meaning to the term "Jeeves." I called my husband Jeeves sometimes as he was always there attending to me. Now, I'm Jeeves, attending to others by taking care of details in order to smooth their passage to the Astral. It's a term of "service with a smile." Jeeves takes charge in a beneficent way.

17 February 1985

Is it hard for you to tell me how you felt when you left your body?

No. I was floating like a dream. Then things got dark and light: dark because the room faded away, and light because the new picture of reality dawned or became clear.

Did you realize what was happening?

No, not at first. I felt like my body was coming along. It took some time to realize that my earth body was no longer with me. There was no pain upon leaving the hospital room, rather a sense of adventure, and a sense that it was right. Yes, it was totally clear that I had to do that thing that I was fearing a little—dying. Be happy about it; be joyous when you know the exact moment has arrived, and go with grace and loving feelings. That's so important, to go with Love, Love for the Universe and for everyone behind, for everyone and everything.

What exactly did you experience?

It was like a film. There was a combined matrix of Love energy coming from everyone I had loved and who had loved me, both on earth and in spirit.

Did you see anyone?

Not right away. Then I saw my grandmother, whom I never would have suspected to see first. She was like a mirror of light, helping me to see myself spiritually and getting me used to not dealing with the body I had left behind in the hospital. By the way, upon leaving, I did see people trying to work on that body. They were doing various things to it. I thought, "How nice, I'm not part of that scene anymore." I felt so relieved and relaxed, but with a respect for the unknown. I moved through a warp of reality, like an airlock on a spaceship, a door or a portal, an opening, like Alice in Wonderland, in no time at all—just an instant.

What did your grandmother say to you?

She didn't say anything. She just looked at me and I knew everything she wanted to say without a word. The message was to relax and enjoy and that she would guide me. She indicated that I would meet my parents at another time.

Have you seen them yet?

No, because they are working on adjustments that are different from mine.

Can you review your past lives?

Yes. I can review my lives and any lives, mine or others, if I desire to do so.

Why did you have to deal with so many physical and health problems in the life just past?

I had to burn off some energy because of my daring nature. There was an imbalance due to recklessness. But I couldn't really be reckless in that life now completed. I wanted to advance and grow.

What was the most significant past life connection for you and me?

We were brothers in a life in Colombia. We were Indians and lived a rural or rough kind of life, being very devoted to each other. Once again, I appreciated your support and caring in this life just past.

3 March 1985

What is the reason for this communication?

To let light into the environment.

What are you doing now?

I am studying the esoteric rules and laws as they pertain to all of my past lives, and particularly to the most recent one. I have to understand more clearly everything that has occurred and my part in those happenings. I am working from a very personal viewpoint now, and am still dealing with the emotions involved. This includes my feelings for all those in vibration to me, both in spirit and in your dimension.

What are you studying?

The Law of Cause and Effect. How infinitely subtle that law is! You only need to wish something or think it for a second for it to be imprinted on your whole energy matrix. It's the same as if you wished for something or thought a thought for weeks or months; the time element is unimportant. Be a guardian of your thoughts! Love the way and intent of the purpose of your life, that is the key. I did not fully appreciate that idea before.

Do you want me to write a book and why?

Yes, I do. It could be helpful for others to have additional viewpoints of the concepts of death—what it really is and what happens when we think we experience it.

Are you content now?

Yes, I am very pleased. I'm happy that we can be in vibration to do some work together. You know the stage was set for this on the earth plane.

Can you tell me about any other laws that you are studying?

Yes, the Law of Inherent Rightness. It is the concept of knowing when and where you are to be at a given point in time. This law can be utilized on many levels. I know this isn't as clear as what I said before. I am studying the idea and looking at pieces of my past lives from the records which are all within my energy vibration. I carry them with me as you carry yours. There are no separate record-keeping facilities in the Universe. You can tune in on the Law of Inherent Rightness with your hunches, your immediate reactions, and your sense of correctness for the variables of a situation. It's a vague idea, but one of the most important in the Universe. It's a law of within, as they all are. Nothing is imposed from without. We work within and with our own energy matrix, as though we were an atom or conglomeration of atoms, ever interlocking, infusing and diffusing. That's who I really am: an energy matrix. That's who you really are too! We house this energy in a body for a while which is a dimension that seems real to us. However, it's not, and knowing this is the most liberating fact of the transition. It's so wonderful to know who you really are. Now, I can feel and think through all parts of myself. My energy systems are all interconnected, radiating and glowing, like a continuously lit up firefly. That's a good analogy, don't you think? (Pause.)

Are we still in vibration?

Yes. These ideas are going to suffice for now. There's much I must contact in myself to be able to clarify and then communicate to you. It's a process as you can understand.

Can you see me physically?

No, I can't, but I can perceive your energy matrix, which is your miniature solar system. Etheric energy is connecting us for these instants to be able to write and to communicate.

Is there any problem with this communication?

No, you want to, which is the key item. That's all that is necessary. Do invoke spiritual protection, as you have done. Then our transmission will always be clear and fine.

How are you effecting this communication?

I am receiving energy support from masters, guides and teachers who act like transformers in an electric power company by revving up my energy so I can communicate. I have chosen to do this work to get the message across to more people: There's no fear to have in regard to death. Death requires a profound respect and a spirit of hopeful adventure; it provokes wonderment, joy and rapture. It is hard to put these feelings into words.

12 March 1985

What are you doing now?

There are a number of things going on for me at the present time. I am trying to piece together all of the strands of my energy gestalt, which is the matrix I spoke to you about before. There are areas of it that are dangling or split off from the main lines and circuits. I have to re-integrate these parts for my level of self-understanding to grow and my eventual progression to another level of awareness.

How did this situation occur?

Through life experiences and inharmonious thinking that drew certain happenings to me. It was my part in the creation, for example, of the physical and psychological problems that I just experienced in this most recent life.

How are you remedying the situation?

By soothing the dangling strands of my energy matrix. By recognizing these strands, I am reviewing the energies and thoughts that caused them to split off. You could compare what I'm doing to a self-massage, but instead of playing with flesh and kneading it like bread, I'm playing with currents of energy. It is sort of like plugging different wires together in an electric circuit box to see what happens. There's a lot of trial and error in the process. Everyone has to do this on the Astral Plane: to work to make oneself whole again after the fragmentation caused by the experience of the physical body. You have to go through layers upon layers. It's like fabrics woven together one way and then another, with pretty little threads thrown in here and there. The pretty threads can be symptomatic of energy deregulations, but, as they are so attached to the whole, it is hard to remove them and examine them without disturbing the entire weave of the fabric. Smoothness of function and integration are what I'm diligently working on. You remember how I was also fascinated with pretty threads in the past life? Well, they are just a metaphor for the vagaries of life, those surges of energy that don't meld with the whole piece of cloth. Don't forget that everything comes in handy—every scrap or shred of knowledge, experience and insight, to the highest degree that it can be.

What is it like to be where you are now?

It's such a great experience! It is so wonderfully enriching, like Superman eating Wonder Bread, and knowing that Wonder Bread is doing for you what it promises, which is building a healthy body in so many ways.

What special things are you doing to integrate yourself?

I'm looking at tiny clips of my lives. In every life in the physical realm, there are loose wires. Every incarnation shakes up your energy matrix. Therefore, you must soothe it, caress it, and re-order it according to your newest understanding of what or who that matrix is. This is a continuous process of refinement which is superimposed on your original energy matrix form created by the All in All. We are trying to do a jigsaw puzzle and fit our concept of the matrix to what it really is. As more and more of the pieces fit, the more wonderful and exhilarating it is! Each incarnation gives us more pieces of the puzzle so that we can blend once again with the total harmony of the Universe. This is hard to explain in earth concepts, but I think you and others can understand what I have just said.

Thank you for this information.

You're welcome. These ideas can be helpful. I had a lot of fears, but more, just not knowing what death or the Astral Plane had in store for me was very perturbing.

However, you never can know exactly what you will experience in death or on the Astral Plane because so much of who we are is submerged in the earth body. Who we are in total determines our Astral experience and what we seek there. Love is again the attitude to have prior to death. Love helps you to start the coming integration process before you leave the body. Any expression of Love is integrating beyond belief. You, Wayne, don't really know that power. You do intellectually, but you have not experienced it in a visceral way. Like many, you are afraid of Love in its purest form.

Can you talk about your other activities?

Yes. You can't imagine how many simultaneous things I'm doing, all within a flash. There are no time constraints here, none at all. I can work as much or as little as I want. I can decide what I'm going to do from moment to moment and switch gears in a millisecond of the mind's eye.

Spontaneous dictation:

Look to your concepts of Self—this I say to everyone. Make sure they are founded on rock solid evidence from within. Know yourself and as Shakespeare said, "To thine own self be true." Any concepts of Self coming to you from others are interesting bits of information, but not necessarily the truth. The better you know the Self, the smoother your transition to spirit becomes. It is almost effortless. Actually it is effortless, but you won't drag your heels and retard the full potential of your transition if you conceptualize yourself from within, not without. What your outer trappings are in physical life are infinitesimally unimportant. Your station of life, your job, your money are all just toys, like building blocks to play with or objects to cuddle with on a cold night. You return them all to the "store" where you got them when you transit back to spirit. Understand that the toys of earth are like a speck or a single atom of the All That Is. That puts things in perspective.

Can I use this information to teach others?

Yes, absolutely. That's why I'm writing to you because you are to teach and I'm to teach, each from our respective planes.

7 April 1985

What have you been doing?

It has been a period of never-ending increase of knowledge and understanding of myself. This is the main purpose of the Astral Plane: to accomplish the knowledge of Self. It is this knowledge that makes it possible to achieve great strides and to rise to the next level of the Astral. There are several, you know.

Can you describe the levels of the Astral?

Yes, I can from my vantage point. You must understand that the Astral is a conglomerate of energy threads (Here I go again!) that intersect infinitely. Give me a moment to consider. . . . The Astral has as its basis the emotional state of those in the dimension. Emotions are the fuel of the Astral, like a perpetual motion machine which never stops the output of energies. So, the emotions carried here from earth plane incarnations fuel the Astral on the lower levels. Indeed, there are different levels, but no distinct ones, so I can't give you a number of how many there are. Although they can be perceived, they can't be numbered. They blend into each other, and where one begins and the other ends cannot be determined in any simple way. Can you understand that?

Yes.

Good. Now, as one discharges the earth emotional energy into the Astral, one also helps to support the energy grid of the Astral while making oneself lighter. In this way, you can climb to the higher levels. Again, remember that there are no highers or lowers here; I just use those terms as a description. You must discharge yourself; you must get rid of all the accumulated emotions in your body battery. I'm talking about the Astral body since you don't have the physical. Even during incarnation, the emotions are stored in the Astral, so that's how you take them to the Astral Plane. Do you understand?

Yes. Why do you have to discharge the emotions?

To be able to integrate your energy matrix as I explained before. If you carry the emotions of past lives with you, you cannot integrate yourself with the All That Is which is a step toward the eventual reintegration with the All In All. So, if you can understand the analogy of a bee, you can see how you dip your stinger into the energy grid of the Astral. However, you discharge your stuff there instead of taking on energy. Some entities do try to take on energy from the Astral grid, but not for long. They get confused and remain temporarily paralyzed with the infusion of uncountable emotions floating on the grid.

Can you continue?

Yes. I'm thinking about what else I can say about this concept. The emotional fuel is what can be utilized to view past lives and light up your circuits so you can internally perceive your personal Akashic records. As I told you, you carry them in your energy matrix. Think about a pinball machine or a game whose board lights up when you score points. If you put the correct wires together, you reward yourself with points. As stated before, this re-integration process is trial and error, but do remember: It is so important to be open to the experience of re-integrating. Many who enter the Astral think they already perceive what or who their energy matrix is. They don't open up to the self-testing that is required to lighten themselves. The lightening toward finer and finer material is what the process is for re-uniting eventually with the All That Is. Therefore, these entities get stuck or short circuited. They may stay for long periods in some self-created corner of the Astral, continually re-experiencing a hardened concept of Self, which may be exemplified by a certain event of the past life or supported by certain similar events in other past lives. It's sort of like a video recorder repeating the same scene over and over. Until they say, "That's enough of this nonsense," nothing else happens for them. This scene, infinitely re-created, could be positive or negative, but, by the way, the terms positive and negative are only in the eye of the beholder. The word negative in earth terminology can be used to explain people's concepts of Hell, because, of course, there's no Hell. What is supposedly negative is only an energy expression, just like what is supposedly positive. That is an abstract idea, but I'm trying to get a lot across today. I will try in the future to clarify these thoughts, but I want to move ahead, because I'm understanding more of the Astral as "time" in your terms progresses, O.K.?

Great. How do entities get unstuck from their hardened concept of Self? Can you explain?

Yes. A thought can change the process, that's all. They

just have to be open to themselves. That's why to know oneself is so important. These entities get caught in how the society of the Earth Plane conceived of them or get caught in the illusion of what that is. So, don't deceive yourself with illusions of earth—go within. People on the Earth Plane have spoken of the need for meditation; it's a good channel for screening out the earth static and getting closer to you.

Did you get stuck on an image of yourself?

Yes, I did. I saw myself as an invalid because so many saw me that way. I saw a scene of myself in a wheelchair over and over, until I got sick of it. I was very attached to the emotions of care, but also to the emotions of pity that others broadcast toward me. I could not see myself as anything but a waif without the power that she wanted. The truth is that I am power; of course, we are all power and energy, nothing more or less. That does sum it up, doesn't it?

How did you personally move beyond that image of yourself?

By getting tired of the scene. I decided, "I can't stand this anymore. There's got to be something else." Then the film loop stopped. I felt more open and drifted into a feeling of peace or a more loving space, if I can possibly describe it to you. It felt like a release from the cares and pities of others as well as those I myself added to the total package.

Did you take on energy from the Astral grid rather than discharging it?

No. If you can visualize a form like an infinite grid, well, that's what the Astral resembles. I know you saw the movie *Tron*. Earth Plane often presents non-Earth Plane concepts—the "as above, so below" idea once again. But to answer the question: I did not dip into those emotional mini hot tubs in the squares of the grid because they seemed repellent to me, like waste materials. I guess I sensed that I had to rid myself of the dross or gross emotions, rather than to gather more, like squirrels do with acorns. I'm glad that I didn't do it because the resulting confusion would not have permitted this transmission to you, as well as other kinds of communication I am using right now.

What other kinds of communication are you using?

I'm using thought transference to some other incarnates. I have chosen to communicate from this realm for my own evolution and the evolution of others on the Earth Plane.

What else can you say about the Astral in regard to emotions on Earth Plane?

Pure emotion can only be experienced on the Earth Plane. Then it must be discarded on the Astral by peeling it off in layers and depositing it in the honeycombs of the grid of the Astral. The Astral Plane is a wondrous environment. A tiny thought has the power of the greatest force on earth imaginable. You must learn to modulate your thoughts on the Astral because the Law of Cause and Effect works in a millisecond, producing whatever so-called reality that clothes the aforementioned thought. Do you conceive of this in your mind?

Yes. Did you experience this thought power?

Yes. I wanted to think of grandiose things at first: a princess in a palace, a hurricane, in order to enjoy the ferocity of its winds, a huge diamond, a well of pure water, an ice cream cone, an exquisite chocolate, or a jet in the sky. All very nice, but I didn't bargain for the intensity that each thought produced, creating the environment which supported the thought in such perfect detail and with such force of energy. It was almost overwhelming because my emotional desires were, and still are to some extent, within my energy matrix or in the Astral surrounding it. So I had to be careful and use thought power more judiciously. But interestingly enough, the desire to open up after I had been stuck on the old tape of the wheelchair image first brought me to grandiose considerations which then took and take me to all considerations. This process helps me to re-integrate those loose wires I've mentioned, the wires of my matrix which are cords of energy woven so strongly, it's incredible. These cords and their function are like a silk pyramid, a spinning top, or a whirling dervish.

Continue. Anything else?

Yes. The Astral is so compelling. It's the best fun you'll have. The work is work, but the rewards are exhilarating. Simply stated, you get to know yourself stripped of all earth images. That is why you must flip through your photo album of incarnations to experience those images once again. Then, you briefly ground them out into the energy grid of the Astral. In so doing, you are eventually left with the pure essence of Self, without illusions. Don't fear the Astral, it's wonderful. Embrace it as you embrace your every incarnation. Go for it; let it into your fiber. There are no boundaries on the Astral, everything blends with variations of color. It's a mottled effect like tie dye or yarns of graduated color. Ah, think of a color on the Astral and you experience it totally. You're so enveloped by it that you're freaked out at first. I know I'm using 1960's terminology, but I was looking at my teen years in the past life, and I'm grounding out that energy by using some of the expressions. You know them too, and my using them helps you to re-connect with your past. Action/reaction, everything is mutual in its strictest sense. Maybe I'm being too vague or esoteric. I hope not.

No.

Good. There is so much to say on the subject of the Astral. There is so much to teach people and to help reassure them by removing their fears and prejudices about the term death. There is no death, only life, and all must know this fact. Life is the only truth of the Universe; nothing ceases, everything IS. On the Astral, you seek to understand and can, in direct proportion to your openness and desire.

30 April 1985

Prior to transition, what can one do or what attitude can one take to assist the process, and, is death a surprise or is it anticipated somehow?

You must be ready for it in whatever format it is going to take. You receive an inner touch, an inner knowing. I am answering your second question, too. So you do know. I knew for a while, not just because of the physical signs which were my illnesses and infections, but on the inside, I knew. Therefore, I had to make peace with some people around me. Make peace with yourself primarily, and that will extend automatically to those around you. Love your essence, sense it, and feel it with all its inherent power. Know that it is there for you on the deepest levels, because your essence is with you in eternity. I use the word eternity lightly because it is a time value and, of course, there's no time. You must relax. Fighting inevitable change is counter-productive. You just slam yourself into a wall by resisting. So relax! That helps those around you, both in spirit and on the Earth Plane. Your friends and family feel lightened by your acceptance of Self and the coming change. Also, the assistants on the Astral, those who choose to work on helping to effect transition, can do their jobs better if you are relaxed and even happily expectant. That's really the correct frame of mind: to be happily expectant. Remember, there is only Love awaiting you. This Love is of the most powerful proportions and is all-encompassing and everlasting as well as being all-enveloping and transcending. The language is convoluted, I know, but I must get across the total power of this Love that permeates the Universe. It's Love of such proportions that Earth Plane entities cannot perceive of its whole dimension. They can only taste little bits and pieces. Don't worry about the process of death. You get lots of support and a number of insights as the process unrolls like a ball of yarn.

Have you finished?

No. There's lots more to say about transition. Just let this amount suffice for now. It takes a while to absorb, simple as the concepts may actually be.

Who tries to take on power from the Astral grid of energy?

Those who loved power on the Earth Plane. They have an unquenchable thirst and a lust, if you will. It has to do with an unrequited desire nature that they can't control. So they must sample the power of the Astral grid, like a wine-tasting party. The difference is that they get burned and shorted out. Then they start responding like Pavlov's dogs, leaving the grid alone. They are injured a few times in this process; however, they can repair and re-build themselves. Interestingly enough, the parts of their matrix that become exposed by the power from the Astral grid are exactly those parts of Self that need to be worked on. It's something that can't be avoided for certain entities; it's inevitable.

How can you utilize the power of the Astral grid to light up your circuits without infusing yourself with that power?

You want me to further clarify the last transmission. Well, you simply desire not to use the power to enhance yourself personally. You desire to use it for Self-enlightenment. It's all in the purpose or reason behind the desire. You do not assume the power of the grid if you only want to borrow it in order to learn. If you desire self-aggrandizement or power over others, the energy of the grid will short-circuit you and thwart you. But if your motives are clear, as they should also be on the Earth Plane, the results are helpful, and, of course, benign. So, just desire to learn about yourself. The Astral grid is a wonderful friend who is very generous to you. It symbolizes pure Love in this way.

What nuance or portion of the Astral will be the starting point for a given entity upon transition?

This is a complicated matter, but I'll attempt to answer according to my perceptions. An individual lives a certain time period on the Earth Plane. Karmic forces are at play and are in the process of balancing the All That Is in that person. The extent to which karmic forces are balanced or not balanced at the time of transition determines the starting point on the Astral Plane. Let's say that Person X has not neutralized his fear of the dark. Naturally, that's one of the first things he will face on the Astral. Overwhelming thought forms from the Earth Plane come with you and you need to face and clear them out first. This basic disharmony or primeval fear might place Person X on a so-called lower Astral level where grosser forms can manifest. This does not mean that Person X isn't karmically balanced in other ways. Therefore, the irrational fear of the dark may be softened or compensated for by other factors. Person X still has to face this imbalance on the Astral and work it out, but working it out may be blended into other Astral experience, rather than Person X only experiencing his fear of the dark and nothing else. Is that clear?

Yes.

Spontaneous dictation:

The transition is fun! Remember, you don't have to be gloomy on the Astral. I just used the previous example to illustrate how individuals might manifest their worst fears. However, they can also manifest their greatest joys. But that can get overworked, too. Balance is the answer. Balance out Cause and Effect on the Earth Plane. Let nothing get out of hand by becoming an insurmountable fear or a too prolonged joy. Be moderate! Now, I sound like Voltaire: "Il faut cultiver ton propre jardin." *(You must cultivate your own garden, ie: yourself).*

Can you explain the term "lower Astral?"

Yes. Lower Astral is denser and higher Astral is lighter. It's like sifting cake flour as you separate the dross or heavier stuff by letting it settle to the bottom. That's why fears can only manifest on the lower Astral; it's gross and dross—a good rhyme!

Thank you for the information.

You're welcome. Again, I have more than this to say regarding these issues. They will come up again in the future, but this will suffice for now.

Is moving to the West Coast a potential for me?
(This personal question is included because the answer is applicable to everyone.)

It is a potential. There are no wrong choices on the Earth Plane. You get hung up in thinking that you must make the right choice. Every choice is a right choice, don't forget that!

9 June 1985

Spontaneous dictation:

It's great to be in contact again. Do not be out of touch so long as it becomes harder to re-establish contact. But we don't seem to have any problem today. Your guides are very helpful. I want to thank them for making the etheric link between us into such a strongly forged bond for the time we have to communicate. Of course, the frequency of contact remains up to you. I do have a lot to say and only a limited amount can come through each time. It depends on your energy vibration and receptive channels. We can't burn your wires with too much at once, you know. Is that fairly clear?

Yes. What are you learning now?

I have so much to share. Well, here goes. Right now, I have been meeting with entities in spirit who have been and always are part of my Oversoul. They are part of the larger entity, which in turn relates in its way to the All in All, or God. Re-connecting with these sparks of the larger entity is empowering. You receive support and verification of who you really are. I've been self-searching, as I told you, via my Akashic records and reviewing all my lives. Now, I'm getting clarification on the beingness of my individual energy vibration from other individual entity vibrations who are part of the same soul group. You could conceive of them as twin souls. Each entity has many, like atoms splitting off from a molecule simultaneously. They all have the same energy properties. However, they go off in different pursuits and toward different dimensions and planes. At times, many of these twin atoms or souls are in the Astral concurrently where they promote and support each other's growth and development. It's like a workshop where similar chords or even identical chords play off one another. They blend their harmonies with the aim of teaching all present in the Astral, as well as those incarnates connected via the same original source.

Are we still in contact?

Yes. I'm thinking of where to go with this information right now. We, as a group, can use our combined energies to get an overview of various dimensions—Earth and others—in order to view those soul mates or twin soul incarnates who are part of our group. We can see their matrices and their learning environments. As a study group, we can encapsulize their learnings and integrate them also into our essences, if we so choose. The choice is always there; you don't have to do anything. The growth potential of all this is magnificent! You can absorb so much on the Astral. While some of what you are learning seems new, you or anyone is just re-acquainting himself with the All in All. Knowledge and experience exist in the All in All forever and in their most complex forms.

Remember this phrase: "There's nothing new under the heavens or moon or sun," or however that goes, but you get the idea.

How long are you involved with this workshop?

That depends on your desire to know yourself. The workshop is designed to move your self vibration to a higher frequency level. However, first, through your own volition, you must step up your frequency to a point of magnetizing the others in your soul group. They are making the same choice, so it ends up to be a simultaneous decision for those at a similar point of development in their self-analysis. All of your twin souls in the Astral will not be involved at the point where you are, only those whose unfoldment and development are in similar vibrational harmony. Those who are more connected and those who are less connected to their individual essences than we are, are not a part of our present process. But since they are part of our group, they can choose to monitor the proceedings, much like tuning in from a distance with a Walkman. Even those incarnates in our soul group can tune in if they choose. They usually do in the dream state, or they may receive enlightenment through conscious mental channels, which come to them like flashes of intuition or insight. The physical and non-physical incarnate dimensions are more influenced by and connected to the Astral or discarnate than one might suppose. The word "influenced" was just stated in its most positive context. Free will reigns supreme on all dimensions; that's real important to remember. There are no forces that compel, but they do impel. It's totally your decision how you react and what you do.

Spontaneous dictation:

The trials of the incarnate dimensions are like paper

tigers. As incarnates, we see them larger than life, heavy with substance, and awesome in their impact. But really, they only provide a framework for learning which is re-connecting yourself with the All in All or universal knowledge, information so encompassing that it is barely conceivable.

Can you give more details about your group?

No, I can't. I can't identify them in regard to incarnate lives—that wouldn't mean anything to you or to a reader of this material. But I know them all. There's a perfect harmony and a glue of Love which magnetizes us. It's so wonderful, that kind of total identification and unfettered Love. The number of entities changes; it's a drop-in workshop. I'm still in it and will be for awhile. I have much to re-connect with. What can I say? The summary word for the experience is "exhilarating" to the millionth power. The photos of the group are immortalized and imprinted upon the general Akashic records of the Universe. I use this word photo to mean "imprint" or "image." We can choose collectively to tune into our beginnings, to any stage of our evolvement, to any dimension or life, if you will, and to any corner of the Astral. All knowledge is imprinted in the Akashic records. It's hard to explain, because, speaking of my group, we're evolved and unevolved simultaneously. Time doesn't exist. This is a confusing concept; maybe I don't yet know how to convey this thought. Let me reflect. This time thing, the simultaneousness of the All in All, takes many approaches or passes to comprehend. The more I dictate, the more I may be able to clarify things. We are dealing with the ultimate VCR, the Akashic records of the All in All. Part of the workshop purpose is to familiarize the participants with the scope of information at our disposal. We are all an integral part of the fabric of the Universal Akashic records! Upon first coming in to the Astral, many entities don't realize this fact. That is why the self-examination process must occur to the point at which the entity realizes his vast inter-connectedness with the All in All. He then starts magnetizing other parts of his Oversoul entity group into harmonious vibration.

21 June 1985

What do you want to tell me about?

The photogenic quality of the Universe. Everything is image, just layers upon layers of images superimposed. It's like when your camera may not function correctly or when it is out of focus and you see blurs. Such is the stuff of the Universe, which is the term I'm using for the All in All. There are blurs because of intersecting points where dimensions or images meet and blend with each other. You can notice this phenomenon in certain energy centers or spots on the Earth Plane. Be more aware of this potential; these fuzzy points of focus between dimensions where the various images superimpose are where you can contact other dimensions more easily. Sensitize yourself to your environment and you will see more—through your third eye and via all body sensory organs. The Universe is so photogenic and beautiful, like layers of wispy etheric matter drifting, but always within wondrous planning. There are no dangling pieces; every tiny atom has its place in the whole of the All in All.

How can one find these points or spots?

These points on the Earth Plane are discernible because they are like the eye of a hurricane. When you sense a stillness, a motionlessness surrounding a quiet with echoing proportions of nothingness, you will know that you have found one of these spots where the dimensions intersect. Then you can, if you choose, expand your present conscious awareness by seeing into other dimensions. Do you understand?

Yes.

These spots can be anywhere, not just somewhere that is always quiet. They can even be in a clattering environment. It does not matter. Just get more aware of entering these zones and you'll find great expansion. Let yourself taste the Whitman's Sampler of Universal dimensions. What you will experience will only be limited by you. You may see "spirit" or you may have a waking dream like the one a friend told you about recently. He was in one of those spaces. There's a corner of his apartment that he has opened to other dimensions where he can see things, or travel through the blurred image where two pages of different scripts touch corners. He has already accomplished this in a dream state. Now, he is trying it in a more conscious state. He is advancing in this way. Get into those special corners more frequently. You will, now that you are more aware! The keys to the Universe are hidden in funny little places like a certain corner of a room, a brook in the country, or even inside a piece of candy, silly as that sounds. All testing is valid to find these spots. Open up to experiencing them in whatever way you choose. Meditate with eyes open or closed. Sharpen your body senses: use all of them. Let your third eye do the walking or seeing (couldn't help that pun). The key is sensing the point of stillness; then, many things can follow from that.

What can one expect to experience in these spots of dimensional joinings?

Nothing in particular, yet everything because there is

the potential of experiencing the All in All. Even a millisecond of almost glimpsing the All in All is so incredibly exhilarating, more than any false Earth Plane stimulant. You can't imagine unless you have at least tried to grab a shooting star.

Do you have any more to say on this subject?

Yes, but what I have said is enough for now. It gives you something to consider. Why do you always sit on the same chair to do this writing? You are in a still spot of the Earth Plane when you're in that chair in your apartment. That's why you gravitate toward that spot. The warp or blending at this point around your dining room table helps facilitate our contact.

Spontaneous dictation:

There is such a well of spring water here; the spring water is information. I can only bring a cup of it to you at a time, enough to quench the thirst, but perhaps make you desire more. The source of this spring water is the well of infinite Love. This information is a condensation of infinite Love. All matter is Love in denser or finer form, because the Universe, the All in All is Love, which is the element that is fleeting on the earth but here reigns supreme.

Thank you, Janice.

Thank you. I think today's writing has food for thought. I want to express my joy and gratitude to you and all who make this contact possible. Love, White Light, and Peace around you always.

8 July 1985

It's been a while again, but that's O.K. You have to be in the right space, but do let's get on with it, Wayne. Just listen to your inner voice because it never fails you, and you will know what you need to do. Stop a second, withdraw mentally from your activity of the moment, and you get an answer faster than you can imagine. I'm not going to be pushy about our communication, but don't forget that in some ways time is limited. I'll have to break this link later due to my own changing needs and growth, but for now, it's part of the regular scene with me. So, let's continue!

Fine. What is the current status of your work with your soul group members?

The current status: My group members have gotten into the concept of fission by combining our individual energy matrices in order to get in touch with a larger portion of the All in All. That's a vague idea, but it has great validity. You see, we are limited in some respects by our scope. Nowhere is that more apparent than on the Earth Plane, but, it's also a stumbling block on the Astral. Via our soul group connections, we have gone over to a larger view. We are nurturing each other into wider viewpoints and greater scopes of all the dimensions that we can perceive. However, even we together cannot perceive all of the dimensions that are. Do you comprehend what I am saying?

Yes.

Good. Now then, our group workshops have been illuminating to say the least. I have joyfully participated and am participating to the best of my ability to do so. I am validating myself and my soul mate group. Taken collectively, we are our Oversoul, which is also considered to be an entity, more diffused though it is.

Can you explain the concept of fission, as you are using it, more clearly?

By fission I'm saying that the expansion potential of our combined matrices is limitless. The only boundaries are self-created. Let's say one entity in the Oversoul group is resisting or somehow stuck in a vacuum. He doesn't perceive and cannot share or sublimate in respect to the Oversoul's total group. That entity impedes the Oversoul and the soul mates in achieving their limitless potential. It has a real dulling effect if some of our brother/sister entities are jamming our total frequency. Therefore, we help each other to get clear and to have a neat and open package in order to act as a channel for our combined matrix of energy. The incarnate parts of our Oversoul can also jam the group frequency, so we all have to work together.

What causes blocks or resistance in a given entity?

These blockages arise out of negative thought, doubt, and other self-created chains and harnesses. So our work together is one of true brotherhood, sharing, counseling and mutual support. These are woven together in a web of pure Love which is the glue of the All in All.

Spontaneous dictation:

My soul group has the effect of an ever expanding wave, a ripple effect. My group moves another, and that one moves another, and so on. The Universe or All in All has through itself manifested this transmission of waves. Thought moves on waves; thought is energy! You have the principle manifested on the Earth Plane as the ocean movement. The All in All is composed of waves of overlapping etheric thought energy. Thought and Love are really synonyms, although you can't perceive that fact on the Earth Plane. Thought is the substance and Love is the means to move that substance. They are really integrated; you can't separate them at all. So, my dear Wayne, that's how the Universe or All in All functions in the most simple terms. The beginning of these waves of energy came from the original Perfect Thought grounded in the original Perfect Love, which is what we define as God. The idea or concept of waves of energy of the All in All relates to the Law of Cause and Effect perfectly. Can you visualize that? One tiny thought carried on the web of Love creates a ripple, a movement that swells ever outward. These movements are not just lateral in the same plane, they radiate in all possible directions, creating combined etheric energy matrixes that can be visualized like a planet. By the way, a planet is a condensed example of the All in All, just as an atom or a molecule is.

What is your present stage of adjustment to the Astral?

My present stage of adjustment? Well, I'm at home. I don't long for the Earth Plane, friends or family, as I did when I first came to the Astral. I have discovered who I am here. What can be more important than that? It is the answer I was searching for on the Earth Plane, but didn't find. You will find it here for sure, although it is possible to find it on the Earth Plane. I learned how the Astral functions and I'm at peace, in perfect harmony and Love. I still have to clear some channels. I'm not always transparent, which means I have some residue from other dimensions. My group work is helping me to clear, to become ever lighter, and to widen my scope. That's why this transmission will stop at a certain point;

I will no longer have the denser vibration necessary to establish a link with the Earth Plane. Understood?

Yes. What do you still have to learn or to adjust to?

I am learning how to best assist others in the beginning of the transition experience. I can aid them. I must respect their karma and their emotionally charged thought patterns when they transit. Basically, they have to work it out, but I can aid them, if they so desire. There are no shortcuts. They have to examine themselves, their short circuits, and their loose wires in order to see how the package fits together and then see more clearly their own potential whole. It's a challenge, because I do want to step in and give information. However, I can't, if it violates their karmic thought designs. But I can offer Love and insight, one piece at a time, if they desire it. My presence and those of others are made known to the transitees. They may actually use us as a vehicle for their emotional discharging into the Astral grid; we show them how to discharge. But again, they must choose to know. There's always free will; there's no coercion from anyone. I'm learning the Astral guide role, which may be defined as an Astral counselor. All who enter the Astral need hands of Love, to guide, to care, and to be there as the opening unfolds. The seed or transitee germinates, then fans his energy outward like a flower opening, like a drop of water in a tranquil pool, ever widening and impinging on and blending with the countless other waves of energy in the All in All. He expands into a limitless potential where there are no boundaries.

Do you have writing contact with other Earth Plane entities?

No, I don't. It is not necessary. You are to transmit this

information; that is enough. My present work is to learn and to share what I'm learning. You are to share this information. It will resonate for those who seek it. You know this to be true.

Are you actively involved now as an Astral guide or counselor?

No, I'm observing others. It is the practicum stage now. Soon, I will be an active guide and will talk about the experience more. I will be able to observe transitions in detail and even experience them, as I aid the transitee. I blend with him or her in the process. You could see it in traditional terms as the concept of an angel guide on the transitee's shoulder. I'm there to comfort and to surround the jangled energies with the substance of Love or White Light. White Light is the conceptualization of pure Love energy, nothing more. The guide position is rapturing. We help transitees to rapture, which is the Biblical word meaning transiting in pure Love, joy, total peace and harmony within the All in All. More on the guide position next time; you've been one too, between other dimensional lives when you've been on the Astral—remember?

Do you have any more to add?

No, I think I've been clear in explaining some All in All concepts. I send you pure Light and Love. Janice.

14 July 1985

What are your responsibilities in learning the Astral guide role?

First of all, I had to make a choice to be an Astral

guide. That is just one of the things I want to do while on the Astral Plane. Of course, I had to want it before the possibility or potential could even start to manifest, just as on the Earth Plane. My responsibilities are two-fold: To ease the shock of arrival while presenting the new arena of toys and games, and to help support the fabric of the Astral as the new entities enter. Their entry tends to throw off the energy balances. I consciously help to offset energy surges and drains that the Astral grid continually experiences as transitees from other dimensions arrive here. Sort of a balancing act; not bad for a Libra or former Libra.

Can you explain how you help transitees?

Yes. I and other guides help coat the transitee in a protective layer, like a mantle of white light. This serves to soften their entry by causing less friction in the etheric and less disturbance to the Astral grid. The transitees feel relieved, not naked, so to speak, because the feeling of this mantle is like being wrapped in pure Love, pure truth, harmony, and perfection. The guides, including myself, thought-create and thought-project this mantle to cover the transitee. See it as a magic invisible cloak. It's a talisman, a protection for the transitee. Some transitees reject this protective cover via free will; they are the ones who disturb the energy harmonics of the Astral grid and we must make up the differences. Again, we, the guides, only need to concentrate and we will have created the energy to balance this problem. It is really no problem, just a section or part of a process.

Are you directly helping transitees now?

Yes. I have just started. In doing this work, I can and must get close to the Earth Plane, sometimes meeting the transitee in process, sometimes meeting them at the beginning of the death experience, or even minutes fore. They feel the guide's hand, soft Love, soft pea..., and the sense of stillness that prevails at passage points between the dimensions. This "silence reality" is a key to the imminence of death. It is rapture; one can hear the harmonics of the All in All within that silence. People call it heavenly music. I help the transitee to feel at ease during the process. His/her spark/soul knows that we are there. If the transitee has great fear, we may assume the guise of a dead relative, not faking or impersonating for poor reasons, but with the permission of those entities in spirit who are said relatives of the transitee. The transitee's relatives/friends may also happen to be guides, in which case they will be the particular guides in question. If it occurs that no one is guiding who is even remotely connected to the transitee, which is highly unlikely, then, another guide, with permission, will assume an identity that the transitee can relate to. This necessity is rare as most transitees are ready to go and do not need the assurance of dead friends and relatives (dead, that is to the Earth Plane). Do you understand these ideas?

Yes. Have you been a guide at other times in the Astral?

No, this is the first time that I have chosen to be a guide to the Astral. That's because I wasn't evolved to the greater scope required to do this work on previous Astral sojourns. I could have expanded more before and have done it, but I didn't. Now, I want to.

Do you make contact with those about to transit from the Earth Plane?

Yes, I have already answered that question. They may see me in their dreams, or they may have a waking dream when the time is near.

Do you have karma with those you help, and how do guides and transitees become matched up?

Guides and transitees have either karma and/or magnetic attraction, which is really the same thing. We may be of the same Oversoul, or from similar Oversouls or origins. Something calls the vibrations together. It's a pull of great magnitude, like concentric circles becoming congruent around the edges for the purpose of the transition event. It's perhaps better explained this way: All entities are like waves of energy; they momentarily blend together, riding on and with each other in a never-ending expansion process. Later, they separate and proceed on their own pathways. If the congruent potential is lacking with a certain entity, I cannot guide his transition.

Do you have any more to say about these ideas now?

No, that is sufficient. I'm just starting in this role, so more next time, as it gets clearer and lighter to me.

Personal question: Why are my sleep patterns so unusual?

Your physical body is awakening, is renewing, is growing in ways not expected by a 42-year-old. By the way, never think yourself old, and you never will be! So simple!

26 July 1985

Spontaneous dictation: 3:45 a.m.

Hello, I send you Love and my fondest greetings. I think this time of day or night is perfect for this communication, because as you thought, there are fewer conscious blocks to jam transmission. The earth vibrations are quieter at this hour. I have wanted for a few days to communicate, but your nervous system has not been in the right space, so to speak. I'm delighted to be in contact now, and, as always, have much to say. When was that ever different?

What new insights on the Astral guide role have you discovered or experienced?

It's a great opportunity to know both sides of a coin, or rather, many sides of a coin, due to the hidden dimensions of the process. Yes, the event or thing we call death is a process, like everything else. It's a process of growth; it's like certain animals who molt or drop their skin when the time is right. We do that too, we drop the physical body to proceed in our growth cycle. The idea is so simple, like elementary school science class. The process of death is not instantaneous. It starts days, weeks, months, or even years before the actual event, depending on the individual and what he creates for himself in his thought process patterns. So you see, dying has its measured time. We start working with the entity as soon as the inner spark or soul mechanism has been triggered via the free will. Dying represents the wish to molt and to move on in cycles of growth. So, we may be working with someone for a long time before their actual transition. A transition is a transmission of energy, just basically a dimensional crossover in simple terms. Love is the basic ingredient of our work. We help the entity to feel the powerful Love of the All in All. They may think that this Love energy is coming from others in their environment, which it is, but we also beam Love to them. Our projection of Love relaxes and eases them toward their own self-made desire to leave the Earth Plane dimension. I have already mentioned the dream work we do. The transitee will probably have pre-cognitive dreams; they may see dead relatives, or be enraptured somehow by the vastness of the All in All. These dreams are to help prepare the psyche, which has been limited to a very narrow focus, to view greater expanses and to prepare for the wide range of freedom of choice on the Astral plane. There, you are the only monitor of your own progress. You may always seek help and teachers to aid you in your growth, but you are the final arbiter of your achievement of expansion of consciousness. Understood?

Yes. What about those who resist the transition?

I'm glad you asked. Those who fight the change and want, via free will, to stay on the Earth Plane cannot, of course. Transition must still occur. The inner spark knows this and decides when in the earth life cycle the change is appropriate, which accounts for the various lengths of life that you witness. The manner of transition, as observed by others on the Earth Plane, has to do with karma. They will say, "so and so died in such and such a way." That is true, but only as far as they can perceive it. The nature of a death is the clothing covering the event, and that clothing and its fabric are determined by the karmic necessities of an entity.

Some transit in accidents. They are prepared on an inner level before the occurrence of the accident. Also, those close to the person are clairvoyantly aware of the upcoming transit. They help the guides to coat the transitee with Love in order to facilitate the slide from the earth dimension to the Astral. Love is the goose grease that helps the slide occur—neither up nor down, but a lateral slide through the dimensions. Some transit using disease as a medium. All ways of death carry karmic impact; the manner, whatever it is, creates a freeing effect for the transitees and those connected to them. Death is an opportunity for liberation. It liberates the transitee from the confines of a physical body as well as liberating the loved ones from confining or limiting thoughts. Remember how the experience of this entity's transit (Janice) changed your scope of consciousness about death? Well, that happens in some measure for everyone still on the Earth Plane when the transitee leaves them. One's consciousness is almost forced to ponder and wonder about transition when one comes face to face with it in his circle of family or friends. So, in this way, people start preparing themselves for their own eventual transition and set the stage for the Astral guides to enter when the time is appropriate. Is all this clear?

Yes.

Good. Do you remember when your Aunt Anna died? She was preparing for a long time and she is one of your guides now. You feel her and the Love that magnetizes her to you. She has done and is doing guide work. She can't communicate this way because she has chosen to do other things. However, she helped you when you were a child to become aware of transition. On the surface you were confused and scared by her leaving, but you felt her Love around you. She helped prepare you then for your own eventual transition. See how early the seeds are planted! Such events of enlightenment could happen in various periods of one's life. It's different for each entity.

Aunt Anna is a guide of yours. Your grandmother Tillie is, too. You feel them now. She and Anna are twin souls, therefore their closeness magnetized and linked them on the physical plane. Tillie and Aunt Anna will help you in your transition, and I probably will, too, even though I'm not one of your personal guides. They send you ever present and never-ending Love; don't forget that Love envelops you always! I bring in the personal references to make a point. Your Life Guides help to smooth the transit, as well as those who are more specialized in the transiting process, like me, or as I will be. Both kinds of guides help the transitee and help each other to help the transitee.

Spontaneous dictation:

The quotient of comfortability re: transition or death has to be raised! The fears surrounding this process must dissolve because they are nothingness, like non-matter. These fears dominate on the Earth Plane; they must dissipate, as transiting will become more frequent due to the coming changes on the Earth Plane. Those entities remaining have a right to feel more relaxed, not as though they have lost something or someone, but as though they have gained! True, they have lost a friend or family member, but they have gained in knowing the plan of the All in All and the potential bliss of the transitee. The purpose of these writings is to heal misconceptions about death and to bring people's conscious awareness to the point of beginning to perceive the vast plan of the perfect All in All. Have no fear of death; there's limitless Love, washing clean the entity and its outmoded thought forms. The dross portion of the entity is cleansed. Then, the pure spark of perfect energy that is each entity can sparkle, shine, and vibrate in the highest frequency possible.

6 August 1985

Spontaneous dictation:

Shall we continue with the information you requested concerning the false concepts surrounding man's thoughts of death and the Astral Plane? Let us clarify the misconceptions that are raging on the Earth Plane in such strong thought forms that not much else can leak through. I send you Love and a mantle of white light, which you feel around your shoulders right now. There is much to say today.

Do transitees ever have foreknowledge of the time and manner of death?

They do not have conscious knowledge of the time and manner of death, but they have an inner knowing. They do sense the imminence of the transition. Sometimes, they even know that it's going to be on a certain day. Perhaps the manner may be clear, too, because the entity has programmed it so definitively. In such cases, the earth events prior to transition underscore and predispose the type of death. For example, someone has chosen to die from cancer; there is much manifestation of the disease for a period of time prior to death, therefore, the manner of death can just about be predicted. Other entities choose not to know either the time or the manner; it's a personal choice issue made on inner levels.

What to do with the remains/the body/the moltings, bury or cremate?

To bury or to burn the molting; it's a dilemma. Both achieve a similar end. The first, burial, re-unites the left-over dross with the physical earth, melding elements once again. The second, burning, releases the energy of the entity more completely and suddenly, blending the remains symbolically with the All in All, rather than with the physical Earth Plane. Both methods form the first part of the Astral Plane lightening process. Whichever you choose depends upon your orientation, be it physical or mental. Go with your comfortability quotient as to which method of disposing of the molted shell is appropriate for you. You choose once again; both answers are correct; it's a matter of personal taste. I wrestled with this problem a lot; I finally felt more comfortable with the earth rather than the fire.

Spontaneous dictation:

The remains in the Earth can confuse Astral transitees who are newly arrived, because they may try to resurrect their earth body in the sense of Astrally projecting it. Because the shell is not totally demolished, there could be a longing to remain clothed in that body. Therefore, they thought-project an illusion of their old body to cover them like a suit of clothes for their first entrance to the Astral. But this can serve a purpose; it can assist both the transitee and the transitors. Having the body still sort of intact on the Earth Plane can be beneficial, because it aids potential thought projection of that body on the Astral, the familiarity of which may soothe the transitee. On the other hand, even with demolition by fire, the body thought form can still be utilized by the transitee, but usually in a glamorized version. The entity who chose to transmute his body by changing its form completely via fire is somewhat freer, but either burial choice gives much the same freedom to change the thought form clothing. Maybe the entity will appear in a body which reflects his concept of perfection. Or perhaps he will be in some other comfortable form, a spark of light? Anything is possible, so I'm speaking in great generalities about transitees. Many choose to thought-project some kind of body covering for their essen... Many choose other forms, or nothing, just the oscillation and glowing of their pure divine essence, which reflects the condensation or distillation of that entity.

What is the purpose of entities who can move or materialize objects on the Earth Plane? Where in the Astral are they operating?

This is a very good question that has stumped many. It is the phenomenon of seances. The entity who can materialize on the Earth Plane has chosen to do just that. Others cannot because they choose not to; they are moving away from earth vibration. The lower Astral entities are hooked, so to speak, like someone on drugs. They love the earth energy, so even thought-created earth energy on the Astral Plane is not enough for them. They want to get really close to the Earth Plane, and are doing so through seances and mediums, like some you have seen. This Earth Plane is addictive. Why do you suppose they manifest things like stones or they move objects? They want to feel connected to the tangible as they think they perceive the Earth Plane to be. These entities who choose not to shed the gross but to hold on to it are in the lower Astral. They can thought-project an object into the physical by using an etheric link with a medium. That's why the object often appears with some force; it was thrown from one dimension to another. Or you can feel heat because of the friction of sliding the object between dimensions. Lower Astral entities do not usually have much overview; they are not very different from psychics on the Earth Plane. They read probabilities and sometimes a little more. When they speak through a medium, they tell you things about yourself that are true, such as your background, to establish a link. Then they read your energy matrix a bit, but not profoundly, because they can't. They are too dross to enter into the heights where a more enlightened perception could be obtained. They give you general information based on your Akashic probabilities. Just a side note, a lighter or more evolved entity can perceive a much greater scope but can't determine your choices either. Therefore, they also can't predict an event sequence with specificity, but they can give illumination on probabilities and their progression factors. The lower Astral is a bridge that must exist! There is nothing negative about it. If there is anything detrimental (retarding growth) in information given by a lower Astral entity to an Earth Plane entity, then that is a function of agreed-upon choices between the two entities in question. There are no victims; we always make a choice in everything. Choose wisely is the best advise I can give to any entity in any dimension. It's not a matter of choosing correctly, because every decision is correct, but wisely, with a sense of appropriate timing.

Can you give an example of karma re: the way someone dies?

Karma around death. Karma entwines in everything, so of course it does in transition, too. The transitee has in his Akashic records lists of propensities and probabilities regarding transition. He chooses which set or combination of sets. The choice fits in exactly with his overall pathway toward regaining the All in All by re-fusing with it. That's the broad explanation; now let's individualize. John X has been on other planets in material and non-material dimensions. He's been on the Earth Plane a lot, too. He has a rich gamut of choices in regard to transition based on his karmic actions and reactions as well as probabilities in all these dimensions. Each set of new probabilities is generated from a previous choice. John X had once desired to manipulate others through sorrow and pity. He often succeeded and was gratified when he did. His present Earth Plane death hinges on these former events. Let's say a relative or one o[illegible] parents manipulates him this time with sorrow and [illegible] He so identifies with these projections that he brings about his death as he is seduced by his own previous life tactics. He feels manipulated, like a puppet on a string. He manifests an illness which results in death, just like one he caused in another via his manipulations. So, all choices have to be neutralized. That is what karma is about; neutralizing action/reaction. The purpose of neutralizing is to be at one with the All in All, the most perfect bliss imaginable!

Why do some entities almost transit, then don't, and return to their Earth Plane bodies? (a near-death experience)

Another good question. It's a choice; they chose to transit, then chose not to in mid-process. Their change, a mid-course correction, has to do with their karma and those around them. Maybe, in order to balance karma, they need more than one death experience in this life. Maybe those around them need to witness this death and re-birth in order to grow and to balance certain of their karmic elements. A conjecture might be that the entity needed to feel the hand of God, that all-empowering Love which is brought back alive to the Earth Plane as a fresher Love. Many of the near-death people return with new attitude and purpose, spreading grace and Love. Their friends and family, too, are more open, loving, and grateful for the return to the Earth Plane of that entity. Then too, walk-ins use this method. Two entities have agreed to share a body and work out individual and mutual karma that way. One leaves and the other enters in the near-death experience. Often that's why there's an energy frequency change manifested as a different personality when the near-death entity recovers his health.

Can you explain the phenomenon of ghosts?

There are no ghosts, just lower Astral entities who thought-project forms, usually themselves. Some people agree with these entities subconsciously to view their thought forms. That is why there is such a variety of so-called ghosts. These agreements can vary in number and be as numerous as the sands of the deserts. A ghost is an energy manifestation; it's the etheric almost made tangible. Lower Astral entities again want to feed their habit of making contact with the Earth Plane. If you don't have an agreement with some entity of past contact to see their manifestation, you won't. Even if you do have such an agreement, you can choose not to see the manifestation. It's up to you. Earth Plane entities can also project thought forms manifested as ectoplasm. They create ghosts, too. So, check in with yourself, with your inner essence. Maybe you are the producer of the ghost or maybe it's an Astral entity connected to you. It has been an excellent session, but let me close as the energy is getting spent. Your guides are tired, too. It's an effort for them to help with this communication, but they do so with great Love for all concerned.

2 September 1985

Spontaneous dictation:

Again it has been a while, but don't despair. This time the delay had a beneficial effect. You felt no impatience with yourself because there were two things happening. I was not readily available due to an initiation process I was in. You were in a state of suspended animation in the sense that this link wasn't really possible for you. Other connections were being made for us both. Is that clear?

Yes. Can you explain exactly what you were doing?

Yes. I was connecting with the All in All in newer and wider ways. In doing so, I became more distanced from the Earth Plane. It's a lightening process, like cream rising to the top of a milk bottle. And you, well, your wires were being re-aligned to adapt to a higher frequency. So that's why we were both unavailable to each other. You knew that on the inside. Always listen to your heart/gut/head (in that order) and you'll never go wrong; your sense of acting with appropriate timing will be impeccable.

What was your initiation all about?

The initiation was as a priest figure, a White Brotherhood service, as I am a member. I became an official guide or transitor for those making transition. Yes, I was already doing this work, but now I sanctioned myself via the ceremony of initiation. Always consecrate yourself to any important task and the positive results will grow in proportion to your dedication to that task.

Spontaneous dictation:

We are having trouble today. It's the gap of so-called time. Let's line it up later; think of questions. This transmission should stop now. Until soon. Light and Love, Janice.

8 September 1985

Spontaneous dictation:

How did you feel after our last session? I know, frazzled and frustrated—not too much, but some. I will explain.

Why did our communication end so quickly and abruptly the last time?

There were short circuits. You almost went out of body. It felt to you like falling asleep, but it was more than that. It was like a miniature experience of death for one split second. That's how it feels, like a whoosh, like a fast falling asleep. Your guides helped to re-establish you in your body. You felt light-headed afterwards, not grounded on the Earth Plane. It was nothing serious; the malfunction had to do with our being out of contact for so long as well as both of our recent re-alignments. The only danger had to do with not allowing your silver cord to become severed. Since there was some probability that it could have been, your guides and I opted to stop the communication. Had the silver cord been cut, you would have had to leave your physical body. We didn't want to stop, but we didn't want to endanger future communication or to frighten you in any way. But now you know, going out of body and death are like having a vacuum cleaner whisk you up into the sack of the Universe. So, actual dying is easy; it only takes an instant; there's nothing prolonged about it.

Was there a real chance that I would have had to leave my body permanently?

Yes, but a slim one. It was a strange set of circumstances, but your guides and your inner self knew that it's not supposed to happen for a while. However, we decided that it was better not to take any risks on choices and probabilities. Anyway, let's do go on and don't be frightened by this information; there's nothing to fear. You know that now, and I sense that you accept that knowledge.

Why is it important to have a ceremony around

death on the Earth Plane?

A ceremony is a ritual, a passage, a celebrati[illegible] grand analogy, a passion, a protection, an opportunity, a super-consciousness. I can continue with many more phrases. The ceremony is Honor, Love, Peace. It shows a respect for life on the Earth Plane and in other dimensions. It is re-affirming both to the transitee and those incarnates still here. The religion, content, or specific words do not matter. The intent of the words and the ritual are important. The ceremony is a conscious recognition by incarnates of the God force in others and themselves. The ceremony around death is a chance to harmonize with the All in All as much as we can on the Earth Plane. The elements of nature are represented at the ceremony in some way. The body is a conglomeration of the elements and the method of burial also calls upon them—earth, air, water, and fire. The flowers present at a funeral represent nature, which is a mini-universe of the All in All's perfection. They are something tangible that we can see and appreciate. Yes, the ceremony is very important on many levels. It loosens the emotional ties between the transitee and his relatives and friends. It provides a dialogue time between them, although the dialogue may seem one-sided to the incarnate entity. The transitee can choose to hear the ceremony and to be present at the funeral. Earth-bound types who need to get things wrapped up in one way or another can tune in on the ceremony, which accomplishes that. The friends and relatives let go in the process of the funeral. This means that the etheric threads binding them to the transitee are shriveled, disintegrating and freeing the transitee to move on, to let himself go. The reasons for the ceremony are many, but the sadness around it on the Earth Plane is not warranted. This focus must change! The transit is joy! The transit is supreme rapture. It is Love in the most powerful sense of that word. Therefore, let the Earth Plane entities change their conceptions.

Don't be sad; you are just sad about the loss to yourself. Be joyous and expectant! Revelations will come to you via another's transit. That happens all the time. See someone else's transit as aiding your growth as well as theirs. Send them off with Love, as though it's the trip of their heart's desire. Be supportive of everyone concerned. The ceremony raises vibrations. It blesses one and all with a shower of pure Love, like tiny white droplets splashing spontaneously and enthusiastically everywhere. Love is manna from Heaven, as the Bible says. No matter what the religion, the symbols of the ceremony are important and the recognition given and the good will exchanged are paramount to the clarity of all. The purpose of the funeral ceremony is to see the individual entity's life in perspective as well as to see beyond the veil and to glimpse the universal All in All.

Is it important for the transitee to have had input into the shape and form of the ceremony?

Yes, it should be to the liking of the transitee in order to be on the proper wave lengths for various results to manifest. So plan your ceremony while you are incarnate. Even if others don't fulfill your desires completely in carrying out the ceremony, having thought-created an etheric vision of your ceremony helps to manifest it at least partially, and again, smoothes the transition. Don't ignore the inevitable transit. Be prepared, but don't dwell on it. Live your life fully every minute. Do love yourself and your essence; in doing so, you demonstrate Love for the All in All.

How do you view the process of a funeral? What is really happening?

I have already made allusions to what is happening. It's a time of letting go. Some cultures do that via tears, some with laughter. It doesn't matter. However, you mu let go, and a funeral is a catalyst provided to do just tha Of course, there's a reason why some sort of funeral ceremony exists in each culture. Some people thought I was morbid in planning my funeral, but doing so gave me more openness, space, and a sense of freedom. So do plan and don't be frightened of your new life and lands in the Astral; there is always adventure and Love. Isn't the Earth Plane an adventure, too? It's just the same on the Astral. The funeral is a time to make new connections in the process of letting go. Consider how positive energy always emerges. Think how the All in All transmutes everything to other forms, even entities, because there's no difference. Think of the breakthroughs in concepts and the growth a funeral brings. There's more to say, but I will stop for the moment.

From where in the Universe's consciousness come the legends of ghosts and the undead?

They represent a negative side, a gangrene, let's say on the Universal thought. These images were chosen by many unevolved entities and are representative of their fears and negativities. Since these ideas exist on the Astral and were thought-created there, they also exist on the Earth Plane; "as above, so below." They are illusions, that's all. The Universe will always have illusions to choose from. Do not support them via your own free will. Their energy then diminishes in proportion to those who deny them. Verbalize your denial by saying, "I don't want to support that illusion." Also, choose not to see movies with these ideas or read about them. Do so, if you want to, but let's say that you are not helping the total evolution of the consciousness of the Universe by supporting concepts of ghosts and the undead. There's an Earth Plane fascination for these ideas, but are they what you really want? Think about it and decide. The choice is yours; there are no wrong choices. These concepts exist for a reason and that reason is choice.

16 September 1985

Spontaneous dictation:

It has been a shorter interval, which is good. We can communicate more often now to finish this dictation so that the information can be disseminated. The subject today is "Willing your Desires." The Earth Plane is a place to practice that; we do it every day on a limited basis. The Astral is where you'll perfect the Will, using it to monitor thought so that the Astral playground does not get out of hand with too many lions and tigers and bears. On the Earth Plane, your Will seems to be submerged somewhere. Often, it appears that interference from extraneous sources is the catalyst for events rather than your Will. That is not true. You will everything that happens to you, within the framework of appropriate cause and effect or karma. Karma is the suit of clothes covering the Will. The Will is a reflection of the All in All. It is not an individual entity thing; it is connected to the All in All. There is nothing easier to understand. Yes, we have latitude with our Wills, but in the larger sense, every individual Will is moving toward and with the good works and appropriate actions of the All in All. The Will is furthermore a mirror of one's energy matrix. The matrix can see its origins in creation via the reflection cast by the Will. You may have thought the Will was difficult to grasp, but it's really quite tangible. The result is that there are never any victims, only perpetrators. We are all perpetrators of events with our Wills. A caution: the melding of Will with desire can produce some "bastard" children. This is indeed a free interpretation; let's make it more concrete. I was a willful person in the last life, but I was never in touch with the nature of this willpower or its source, which is God. It was not only my Will, it was His Will too. I exercised Will in serpentine and hidden ways on the Earth Plane. On the Astral, all is exposed and open. Your Will hangs free like a movable sign attached to your energy matrix. In the Astral, you recognize your Will right away and you deal with it directly. You can see how imbalances in the intensity of the Will or in its intended purpose can produce monsters. Please don't create monsters on either plane, Earth or Astral. Use your Willpower judiciously, for the good of all concerned. Use it openly; get in touch with your motives and the ramifications of your decisions re: Will-flexing. The Will is the focus of masculine power principles. Admit your use of the Will rather than pretending that you're not. However, be careful what you ask for, because your Will has to be clear. The manifestations of the Will are proportional to one's clarity in Will-flexing.

21 September 1985

Do transitees have problems in transit that you haven't yet described?

No, not really. However, letting go of the desire to be part of the Earth scene is the biggest hurdle to overcome. Focus on your own change/transition just for a brief second and you'll see how you will have to let go of Earth Plane desires. You have to exercise your Will in order to let go, not out of feeling forced to, but out of a sense of rightness. Remember the Law of Inherent Rightness? Your inner self knows that you must let go of the Earth at a particular split second of time. Use your Will to support the plan of the All in All. Let your symbols of material comfort go. The Love of the Universe is greater comfort than any material thing could ever be. Enjoy your objects, but detach; enjoy people, but detach. In do-o, you will transit quite easily and not like a tooth being pulled from its socket.

Can you clarify the statement, "Don't create monsters on either Plane, Earth or Astral?" Were you speaking to incarnates or Astral entities?

I was speaking to both. As above, so below; as below, so above. Either group can create monsters or negativities. Then they appear in the other Plane in Earth dreams and Astral wakings, either way. Again, monitor your Will which monitors your thoughts and there will be fewer monsters to deal with on a daily basis, fewer negativities on the universal Akashic photographic plates.

Spontaneous dictation:

Dreams: Earth Plane entities choose among the symbols that exist—every possible combination of symbol for communication; a dream is communication from the Oversoul to its part—you, the incarnate entity. The Oversoul can beam programs to you or you can beam programs to it—a two-way street. Your dream symbols teach you much if you pursue them. Do write them down, look at them, and analyze them, more for the feeling they provoked than the actual symbol. Love your dreams; they bless you. Have no fears; if you see monsters, you choose to. Look for the reason; you created them or your Oversoul connection on the Astral did. Any symbol has to do with you, the Oversoul and things you must resolve between you. The word is internecine, which means conflict. Also, the symbol has to do with things you must resolve with the All in All, the larger picture. It's a question of inner and outer resolution of issue—simultaneously. You and your Oversoul communicate reciprocally with constant pulsations of information via the silver cord which stretches between you. You have to look at this communication link and see how it works for you. Sometimes you choose to astral-project while asleep to momentarily rejoin your Oversoul. You get pulled up and out of your physical body while the cord stays attached to it. The cord is an etheric link between you and the Oversoul. You use it as a conduit for information and as a means of transport to the Astral. Sometimes you stay in your body in a dream state and images are fed in from the Astral. They are images that you are choosing, but which already exist. Sometimes you go to the Astral and create your own images there with your specific special brand or twist. The dream state is an exercise in masculine/feminine principles. Staying in the body=passive; going to the Astral to create=active. Dreams are a way of sorting out illusions. They give you tools and clues to open up hidden treasures. These treasures are measured as your full potential, which is the maximum output in kilowatt hours of your energy matrix. What you see on the supposedly solid Earth Plane is an illusion. Neither dreams nor the waking state are more real. They both offer clues to reality, but they are distortions, even if they be harmonious distortions. The Earth Plane suffers in the translation of thought to the concrete. While individual pieces are perfection reflecting the All in All, the whole wobbles at times with mis-directed or uncontrolled Will and/or Desire of incarnates. We create distortions here to play with. There is space for this phenomenon in the All in All as even distortion is its own form of perfection. The amount of distortion is proportional to the degree of illusion operating in a given sector or situation. Think about the illusion, clear it out and distortion clears out. Eliminate the illusions by looking at the essence. Ask yourself, what is the real energy focus of the situation? Denude the illusion; strip it of all veneers. The dream state gives us an opportunity to get to basic symbols with few illusions or trappings. Look for the underlying symbol in Earth illusions and you'll find clarity. Ask your Oversoul for clear pictures of the real thing.

Should we always try to keep Will and Desire separate?

Yes and no. Will and Desire do not mix easily or sometimes well. Desires are fun to consider; they form a basis for creative thought and a motivation for action. Desires have to be clarified, with the illusions stripped away in order to then harmonize with the Will side of the equation. Desire is an attracting or feminine principle, so it corresponds to Will (masculine) as the counterpart or balance. If your desire nature is pulling in confusion, which may manifest as negative influences, your Will can create some painful situation. Yes, it will manifest the desire, but with strings attached like thorns. Therefore, examine Desire, streamline it like an art deco locomotive, put it on the track of Willpower, and send it out to be manifest. Get conscious of this process and you will advance your understanding of Self and the Universe. Don't blend Desire and Will unless both have been dealt with. Clear altruistic Desire functioning together with direct unencumbered Will equals beauty, harmony, and grace, which are the reflection of the All in All in vibrational motion. Take care, my friend. Light and Love permeate the Universe in ever-increasing quantities.

25 September 1985

Spontaneous dictation (1:40 a.m.)

This is a good time; there's not much interference about in the cosmos as man has gone to sleep more or less. So, we can communicate clearly and with a surety of not being jammed by other messages and electrical pulsations. The etheric link between us sets up an electrical pulse, if that can be pictured mentally. This pulse is the mental translated to the physical. You have six to eight weeks more to complete this writing. We will know together when it is done. There will be ample warning and conclusion time.

Are we, as incarnates, most likely to have strong rapport/relationships with entities that are also part of our Oversoul, or are we likely to have conflicts with them?

Great question! Let's define the concepts of twin souls and twin flames. There are many twin souls which come from or are part of the same Oversoul. There is only one twin flame for each entity and it is also from or part of the same Oversoul. There's a difference between twin souls and twin flames in number and quality. The quality difference is that the twin flame is in exact harmonics with you, like your congruent other part. It makes up all the qualitites of opposites missing in you, and you make up all the qualities missing in it. On the other hand, twin souls have similar harmonics, some of which may be congruent and some not. The principle of attraction (opposites attract) especially works with twin flames. You are the same energies at different ends of a spectrum. Each of you alone is the All in All. Both of you together are a larger inclusion of the All in All. Twin flames are like two pieces of a puzzle fitting together and solving itself for those two entities in question. Coming into contact with the twin flame makes each one total and complete. You really notice the harmonics with your twin flame, although you may be opposites on certain levels. With twin souls, there's more variety possible. You are attracted to each other, sometimes very strongly, but opposite factors may frequently (but not always) cause conflict. This conflict has the effect of making the Oversoul more aware of parts of itself. That is the greater purpose of having contact with a twin soul: The Oversoul comes to know itself whether via conflict or harmony. Contact with twin souls may be long-term or not; sometimes these relationships dissolve and disappear, depending on their purpose. You may have twin souls for lovers, but differences will be noticed. With twin flames, there are only two of you in existence rather than many. The incredible attraction often links twin flames for lifetimes on the Earth Plane. Indeed, they are always linked in the cosmos for so-called eternity. You can notice both harmonics and conflict with either group. There can be conflict between twin flames if they choose to experience each other that way. A whole experiencing its parts can do so via harmony or conflict. Let's say it's an agreement with yourself. Your twin flame is part of you and vice-versa.

Is your twin flame on the Earth Plane or in spirit?

My twin flame is in spirit also. The name is Bashkir in the best translation I can give. We are working in different levels/areas but we have constant rapport by thought. This thought fosters mutual growth and mutual expansion.

Who is the real perpetrator of a dream, the Oversoul or you? If both, what determines which one will initiate the dream?

The dream maker (maker, remember Dune?) is you, the individual entity. You may ask the Oversoul (your higher Self) to contribute to the dream process, with you being the passive receiver of carefully chosen images/symbols. You chose and the Oversoul delivered, like a pizza takeout of your special order. Or you can create the dream totally on your own, going to the Astral while asleep and playing with the symbol toys in the kindergarten of the

All in All. You are the perpetrator of a dream and v
you see is what you want to see. That's the core of it

Do you have anything further to say about dreams?

Just that dreams are nuggets of gold. Mine them with care and you will see the sparkle of pure Truth, pure Light, and pure Love reflected endlessly in the mirrored ball of the All in All. Enjoy your dreams to the maximum!

Spontaneous dictation:

You have met many twin souls, some just for minutes in your life. The numbers of them are large for a given entity; it depends. Three thousand to five thousand might be incarnate at one time, sometimes up to ten thousand, but usually not more. Meeting them is almost like meeting yourself.

28 September 1985 (no electricity due to Hurricane Gloria)

We are again in communication, but at a time when there's absolutely no interference to the electrical pulse between us. It is to notice; no electricity quiets the environment tremendously as well as quieting your individual energy vibrations. You don't have to play off or play with the pulsations that modern society has placed around you via electrical service and all that implies. It's quite a different feeling, right? The Hurricane Gloria is a sign of shifting energies. The illusions that certain people had that nothing dramatic could happen in New England weather-wise have been shattered. Now, they see it can happen; consciousness has been opened. It's a preview of coming attractions. Weather patterns will continue to change as the consciousness of the planet shifts towards its new pattern to be established some years down the road.

Do we have more than one Oversoul group?

No, you only have one Oversoul group. You are asking because it looks like disparate personalities are in it. Yes, the details of who they are are disparate and conflicting, but there are basic underlying harmonies, intents of purpose, and energy waves that are the same for all those entities. You karmically involve yourself with other Oversoul entities, too. You can have rapport with them and strong connections. However, there's a missing factor; it's an underlying poof, so wispy that it's hard to catch or isolate. This poof is like a signature perfume fragrance that all of you wear in a particular Oversoul group. You only perceive a hint of it as you make contact. That fragrance is part of the attraction principle glue between you.

Are you and I part of the same Oversoul?

Yes, we are part of the same Oversoul. That's how this communication can happen. I'm using your silver cord, or rather we are, to transmit the pulsations coming across in the writing mode. So yes, a twin soul am I. It's not surprising. The twin souls will always give you a clue in some fashion or other.

What general information do you want to share today?

The importance of Light in your life. Light is a symbol, a symbol of the All in All. The sun is a beneficent energy, giving life in this illusion we call the Earth Plane. Go out, seek it and bask in it. The sun is a metaphor for the All in All's protection. Seek Light, mentally create it, see it around you in your environment and so forth. Why? Because you set up growth with Light, your growth and everyone elses. Be sensitive to the mental charge of Light; it puts events of the pathway of evolution rather than retrogression. It only takes a second to see Light in a setting or surrounding a situation. In doing so, you offer the situation more definitively to the careful consideration of the All in All's plan for it. Harmonics are increased, conflicts diminished and oppositions come together on their spectrum by using the Light. The Light is a really important principle. Surround transitees with it mentally. It is synonymous with Love. You often write Light and Love in the sign-off of a letter; you're saying the same thing twice. Surround anything you want with mental Light. The Bible calls it divine protection; it is, but perhaps divine process is a better term. "Let Thy Will be done." "Thy Will" is the thought of the All in All.

Spontaneous dictation:

My energy is low today; it is almost exhausted for now. I accumulate energy much like a metal spring winding up. Then it is spent in the course of communicating with you. Love and Light on your life and setting. Janice.

5 October 1985

Spontaneous dictation:

The connection is strong today. Do you feel the spring mechanism energy as it impinges on your hand? I've wound it tightly to be able to answer your questions. I feel very happy, which I'll explain. So, let's shed some Light here, that's the purpose.

How does an entity assess when it's time to leave the Astral?

An entity knows when it's time to move to another dimension because the Astral becomes uncomfortable. It's old stuff and you don't match with the energies of any corner of it. That's the test: Are you in synchronization with your environment? If the answer is negative, you will seek another dimension where you are. There's a parallel on the Earth Plane: Suppose that you no longer have anything to learn karmically in a certain city or place—you move. Or suppose that you no longer have anything much to learn on the Earth Plane—you transit. These are models of models which are equivalent in nature and design. When the Astral ceases to be a learning tool, you say goodbye and move on. I'm pleased to say that my work with transitees as a guide will continue, but my scope and learning arena will be moving out of the Astral to another dimension.

Is there a general next direction or focus after you have left the Astral?

Yes, there is. The next focus after the Astral is what we call the Meridional Plane, which is where meridians of energy gestalts or Oversouls intersect and interact. It's the general Oversoul Plane. My being there has to do with my closer identification and realignment with our Oversoul. You see, I'm moving on. I can still use the Astral as an adept because I must in my guide work, but soon I will no longer be an identifiable segment of the Astral. The Meridional Plane is a higher ray or vibration. The Oversoul learning and interaction mainly takes place there. The lower planes are for the Oversoul's interaction with itself, including the Astral.

Is the Meridional actually a level of the Astral?

No, it's another dimension. Of course, there are connections and passageways between all dimensions. You must have the key to pass from one to another, but you already do. It's in your own energy matrix. Through self-discovery, you find the key. On the Earth Plane, it works the same way. You find yourself by unlocking another realm of inner consciousness which then becomes outer.

What is the nature of the work that has to be cleared on the Astral?

Besides regulating your emotional excesses, you must clear your energy channels as I mentioned before. You soothe the loose connections and massage yourself, if I can use that metaphor. You need the experience of the Astral: to discipline your Will-power, to learn how to really monitor your thoughts, to clear desires before transferring them to Will and manifestation, and to learn the Laws of the All in All, such as Cause and Effect and Inherent Rightness, which are two that can be more easily understood on the Earth Plane. Therefore, you have lots to do on the Astral. You must work with your matrix, which corresponds to physical on Earth, and with thought, which corresponds to the mental plane. Of course, the mental is the key to your work as all is mental. All is thought, and everything else falls in place by knowing that truth.

Do you have anything else to say about the Astral in general?

Yes, I do. The Astral is not so confusing. You are the final arbiter of your experience there, don't forget. Therefore, think about your true essence while on the Earth Plane. You know what you have to work on, so start now! Then you won't flounder for awhile on the Astral, as many do. There are those entities who stubbornly resist knowing themselves and therefore knowing their Oversouls, which you must do in order to be on the path to rejoining the All in All.

I have lately been attracted to the color gray. What is the significance of that color?

The color gray is the color of the new age. It is an amalgam of the forces now in vogue, which are the forces of change and blendings of energy. Gray represents a blend rather than a total change or shift. You and others are drawn to gray. It soothes entities who are not so aware of the changes and shifts in motion. It's a symbol, it's an alignment tool, and it's a tranquilizer in a very positive sense.

Spontaneous dictation:

The combined matrix Love of our Oversoul beams toward you now. You can feel it like waves of caresses. Love, Janice.

13 October 1985

Is there a different quality today to our connection?

Yes. The energy between us is not different, but your electromagnetic system is. Your energy matrix is more refined and more capable of dealing with this writing process. It all feels more relaxed to you. That's a correct perception on your part.

Is there any information about the coming Earth changes that you want to include in your communication with me?

Others have spoken in detail about the Earth cha that are projected from now until the year 2001, so I not. However, I do want to say that the Astral wil. be very busy. It always is, but, as more entities choose to transit by using the Earth changes as a catalyst, both the population here and the work of the guides will increase. But, we are ready and can handle the work load! The reincarnational process will speed up also, again as others have said. The birth process will not be the only way of returning to the Earth Plane in the near future. Entities will choose to materialize and will be able to. Up to now, they couldn't. Those incarnate on the Earth Plane will more actively choose when to go to spirit instead of being unaware and waiting. I'm not speaking of suicide at all! The choice to transit will be more conscious, that's all. There will be freer access between Earth Plane and Astral Plane as the projected changes open dimensional pathways. Materializing and dematerializing or corporation and decorporation will be relearned. These concepts have been known on the Earth Plane before. As stated, thought creates anything instantaneously on the Astral. Gradually, the Cause and Effect nature of your thoughts will become more and more noticeable on the Earth Plane also as the development of the next time frame sequence unfolds.

You said you weren't speaking of suicide, but of dematerializing. Can you explain?

Suicide is self-hatred rather than self-love. One's energy matrix is totally jammed by that experience. The entity then has to clear figuratively for eons in order to re-integrate himself with Love. I was speaking of dematerializing when the time is appropriate for transiting to the Astral, and not of doing physical harm to yourself to accomplish this end. You, the Earth Plane entities, are becoming more aware of when you have inwardly chosen to transit. You may leave your remains behind or decorporate them, using them as a thought-covering on the Astral, until such time as you don't want to. Then you'll molt, giving that thought energy that was your body to the All in All, which is your larger Self.

You're saying that entities may be appearing and disappearing with some regularity. Is that correct?

Yes, they may. But again, it's individual choice. Even now, bodies may disappear, depending on how the entity has chosen to transit. Some people choose to disappear by means of what we call an accident, leaving no identifiable remains. This happens now, but will happen more in the future.

What else do you have to say about the slated Earth changes?

The Earth changes are not set in stone. They are fluid, subject to the Will of this living entity, planet Earth, as well as the Wills of the entities incarnate on and below the surface. There are other entities in parallel dimensions on the Earth Plane, as well as all the time periods that ever existed which form a congruent whole. Other entities are not visible to you, as they are in etheric form. They are not of the Astral; they are incarnate on the Earth Plane as you are. There are different foci on the Earth Plane for the potential of richness of experience. Whatever specifics the Earth changes manifest, they will bring all the incarnate dimensions more into contact with each other. There will also be more contact between all incarnates and the spirit entities of the Astral Plane. There will be more positive "ilalization" which means "to go in the direction of closer vibrational harmonics with the All That Is." This term describes lighter vibrational frequencies where masters operate.

Positive "ilalizations" refer to the All That Is ascending and becoming in total flow and vibration with the All in All—God. You may not know the term, but it's correct.

What new subject do you have today?

The concept of the Law of Choice. The Law of Choice always gives you the option of movement. You are never blocked in any way, even if you think you are. A choice of nothing is a choice and works in conjunction with Cause and Effect. This law is the basis for the continuous motion of the All That Is. There are split second choices made by all sparks of the All in All with such rapidity that it is incomprehensible. This constant choice is like the beating of the heart of the Universe which provides the movement of the everything that is always in motion. The Law of Choice fuels the perpetual motion of the All in All. Will you choose to drink a cup of coffee in the next few minutes? All of the action inherent in that choice is fascinating to consider—the Cause and Effect. Choice is a precursor to Cause and Effect. Choice is part of the Desire/Will process, fitting in between those two. Desire/Clearing → Choosing options → Will/Manifesting; this is the process. Choice is a very simple Law, but one of the most complex, too. Without Choice, the All That Is would be static, which it can't be by definition, as Choice is an irrefutable Law. Ask for guidance, put your choices in the light, and choose wisely, then you will be in the flow of harmony's perfect plan of the All in All.

26 October 1985

Spontaneous dictation:

There will be two more sessions after this one and they will conclude the book. Today we have details to clarify.

What is the difference between the "All in All" and the "All That Is"?

The ALL in ALL is ALL. The All That Is is a more tangible representation or any tangible manifestation of the All in All, such as etheric matter or physical matter. The All in All is all-inclusive. The All That Is is somewhat smaller in scope because it is defined as tangible, even if that tangibility is hardly conceivable on the Earth Plane. This tangibility is parallel to the concept of the All That Is. It is something that one could define as provable in some dimension. However, the All in All, or God, is greater than that. It is the sum total. The All in All includes all potential latent manifestations of the All That Is, but is as great or greater than the All That Is. Now, have I muddied the waters or are they fairly clear?

They are clear.

Good. I have to really try to translate this concept to the Earth Plane because it is vague, but hopefully, the reader catches it.

Can you explain more about how other entities are incarnate and not visible to us?

They are in other dimensions which are also Earth Plane dimensions and not Astral. The Earth holds several dimensions, the one you operate in and call reality and two more. There is the dimension of the nature sprites or devas and the one of the mineral and plant entities that make up planet Earth. Every plant, every rock, everything on the Earth Plane is an entity operating in its own dimension. The devas or sprites can perceive you, but you can't usually perceive them. This will change as awareness grows. You see plants and rocks as objects but can't see the interactional quality of their functioning within their dimension. The devas ha developed civilization using remnants of ancient o such as Lemuria and Atlantis. They may live on inner or outer earth. Likewise, the plant/rock dimension of entity interaction may be on either inner or outer Earth. Man can't conceive of living in inner Earth, but may do so in the future. To accomplish this, he will use decorporation or widening of the spaces between the apparent molecules that make up the physical body. There is to be greater development in all incarnate dimensions and a regained connection between the three. This unfolds in the next ten-year time sequence of events.

Are the devas and the plants/rocks really part of the same dimension?

No, devas are separate beings; however, they are strongly connected to the plant/rock dimension. They already have exchange and interconnection. The man entity is cut off from the other two, but will be reunited. It is happening already, The deva and the plant/rock dimensions of incarnation have been consciously remembered at Findhorn, Scotland. Now the remembrance spreads to distant lands and greater numbers of man entities.

Do entities of the deva and/or plant/rock dimensions transit to the Astral in the same way as man?

They decide more consciously than man in regard to transiting. They know where and when they have learned the maximum possible on the Earth Plane, and then they leave. It's a conscious choice. Their life spans are not governed by thought manifestations, but by Universal Mind; there are no preconceptions about the length of time possible in incarnation on the Earth Plane. Therefore, the time span of their incarnation varies much more than man's. There are guides available also for their transit, but it's easier than for man, because these dimensions have been throughout thought or eternity more connected to the higher planes: Astral/ Meridional/Master and beyond to the All in All's source, which is the Godhead or spark of ignition. The image that you have in your mind is an accurate one: a sprouting fountain of water or fire. Somewhere in the column of that fountain is the spark of ignition that began the All in All. It is creation and the beauty that implies and is.

What concept do you want to speak about today?

Let us talk about the leading of souls/entities and the leader, which is Christ Consciousness. This consciousness is the incarnation of White Light, which is a pure reflection of the Godhead without dross or interference. Christ Consciousness is a potential for every time and place. I spoke before of putting things or events "in the Light." Go a step further now. Meditate on what the Christ Consciousness is. Then, let that beam shine through you as its incandescent power of illumination shines Light on your path and those around you. Do believe in it! It is ever-present and has been entering the world in greater quantity and quality since Jesus, the incarnation of the Christ Consciousness, walked the Earth Plane as a male entity. Let Christ Consciousness manifest through you. Think of the Lord's prayer: "Thy Will be done, in Earth as it is in Heaven." It is a question of thinking and doing. First, think White Light around a situation, then the potential of manifesting Christ Consciousness in the doing surrounding that situation is activated. A purification occurs; awareness manifests as to every minute detail of the situation. The connection with the All That Is and, therefore, with the All in All is recalled. The All That Is, which is symbolized by the situation in question, is the pipeline to the All in All. Be a Christ figure, not for any ego gratification, but as a channel for the highest good and the positive pathway of manifestation. Let Christ Consciousness enter you! You feel atonement when you do; it's an incredible synchronization!

Do you have any more to say on this subject?

Not for the moment. My energy feels spent because it's such a gossamer concept, but oh, so vital. I send you Light and Love and all inclusive Christ Consciousness. Janice.

9 November 1985

Spontaneous dictation:

It's been fun working with you and illuminating for us both. I have been able to serve a purpose and to fulfill a contract with myself by doing this writing and helping to put spiritual ideas into the light of consciousness.

Why can't I think of anything to ask you today?

Because you are leaving the channel open for a manifestation of knowledge and information. Your thoughts and expectations for my answers could block the information that will transmit today.

What do you want to talk about?

Color. The colors of the spectrum indicate levels of the All in All—as above, so below, once again. Much is known about this already on the Earth Plane. However, I o re-emphasize how the colors you choose and have d you solicit the calling of guides corresponding to the planes relating to those colors and facilitate various dimensional crossovers. Color is a manifestation of heavenly harmony. Gold is the color of the pure essence of the ascended masters. They use gold as a picture piece or viewmaster to peer into the cosmos. If you have gold in your environment, you call on master vibrations. If you have red, you call on entities of the Astral Plane to be in your environment. If you have blue, you call for attention from your Oversoul. If you have green, you seek the All in All's perfection, manifested as health and wholeness. These are the main colors that connect with spiritual realms. Knowing this information is an aid, nothing else; there is no secret formula. Now, when you choose a color to wear or to have around you, know that you are contacting and connecting simultaneously with the spiritual purpose of that color.

Can you give any more details about the colors you just mentioned?

Yes, I can. Gold, as worn in jewelry, brings you a master's touch. Red keeps you in contact with your subconscious and past. Blue calls you to consider new vistas and wider dimensions. Green unites and completes. The other colors all play balancing roles among your individual energy vibrations. Have you noticed being attracted to certain colors for shorter or longer periods of time in your life process? Follow your instincts! You are balancing your energy matrix and your karma by doing this simple thing: choosing particular colors at particular junctures in time.

Spontaneous dictation:

For your pleasure, wear white and you bring happy

vibrations into your consciousness. White is the es of Lightness, reflecting White Light, supporting its p ence. Black steadies. There is nothing negative abou It can provide direct access to yourself, acting as a co duit from you to you. You being attracted to yourself is represented by black. Gray is the balance of truth, symbolized by the blending of you (black) and the other (white). Purple is a regal color. It is the shade of blue given to the higher consciousness as manifested by the concept of the Oversoul. Use it with discretion; it is powerful. Brown is for experiencing the other Earth incarnate dimensions. It calls you into contact with devas/rocks/plants and it harmonizes you with the Earth Plane.

Let color enter your heart. Skip with it, play with it, enjoy it. Think of a formal French ballroom in white and gold. It represents the highest fun: masters cutting a rug. Why do you think that these colors have symbolized the peak of good times and prosperity? Let color blend with you. You are all colors of the spectrum. Your energy matrix is no dull thing; it shines and sparkles like precious stones with all colors and hues. As you enhance your environment with color, you enhance yourself. Enjoy this toy of the Universe and see yourself as the colors that you are. Be a color chameleon as you emphasize various parts of Self. Be a kaleidoscope and refract. Be a diamond as you beam White Light from thousands of facets of your essence. Be a diamond, glowing blue and white, as your Oversoul transmits Christ Consciousness through you to this sphere. Have a physical diamond to help you focus on this manifestation. Women usually do, but, surprise, men should too! It is a stone of the highest order.

How do you feel about the fact that the one year anniversary of your death on the Earth Plane will be in a few days?

I know not of that. The anniversary of my life is here and always here. Death, as conceived on the Earth Plane, must be erased from the illusionary consciousness of man. So the anniversary date is no trauma. It's a joy remembered or always experienced. I can review it, and in so doing, have the experience again.

The energy and this labor are closing down. The next session will be the last one. I'm radiantly happy and loving every second of my existence. Soon, I'll be on the Oversoul Plane and my work will begin there. Light, Love, and Peace always. Janice.

28 November 1985

Spontaneous dictation:

We are in vibration, but it is as hard to establish the link as it was at the beginning. True, there is now a different qualitative nature to the difficulty because we have come full circle. It is time for a completion to our endeavor.

Do you have anything further to add about the concept of colors?

No, I have stated what I wanted to, but do use gold to raise your vibrations as you harmonize with the masters through said color.

What do you want to discuss?

Never limit yourself! Never say, "I can't!" When you use a negative, you inhibit probabilities and possibilities stemming from probabilities. Don't put the brakes on; let your vehicle drive you to the farthest reaches of your potential. Let it move at fullest speed to bring you to the goals chosen prior to incarnating. Have a quartz crystal in your possession. It opens channels and speeds up your vibrational frequencies, which promotes your spiritual understanding and growth. Therefore, buy one or two; have one in your bedroom and one on your person, whether in jewelry form or not. Quartz is a battery of universal Love, storing and projecting it simultaneously, much like the movement of electrical current. The quartz is a radiant elemental being in the sphere of the plant/rock dimension.

Let Love into your environment! See its existence in everyone and everything. Help it to manifest. Think Love. Ask yourself, "How can I approach a given situation with Love?" Love is another word for Christ Consciousness. This book must end on the simple fact that LOVE IS. IT IS in all levels and in all dimensions. Love is the All in All. It permeates your soul/energy matrix. Choose to see and experience it. As you ride the energy waves of Love, you move toward fusion with Limitless Light and Love, which is the glorious ALL IN ALL.

Spontaneous dictation:

Love, Light, and Peace in your time on the Earth Plane. Thank you, Wayne. We will meet again in spirit and in future incarnation.

Love, Janice.

Thank you, Janice.

Love, Wayne.

AFTERWORD

Wayne Hatford does such a good job of explaining how this book came to be that any third-party preamble would only stand in the way of the reader's enjoyment. Now that you've read this far though, it is worth pointing out that *Letters from Janice* is typical of a new, healthy trend in trance mediumship: While communication with discarnate entities is hardly taken for granted, it's finally been stripped of enough awe and obfuscation that we, the living, can get down to exploring the *really* important question of life after death.

Indeed, ever since the explosion of "channeling" in the late 1970's, the darkness of the seance room has become obsolete—as has the seance room itself. Discarnates cheerfully manifest themselves in lecture halls and auditoriums, where the fluorescent lights stay lit. Seminars with Lazarus, Ramtha, Bartholomew, James, and other trance personalities pack in many hundreds of people, and—significantly—most of the audience's questions focus on the hassles of the here and now: How can we maintain good health, avoid negative belief systems, achieve peace, increase personal creativity, and dope out the tricky, ever-beguiling paradox called Life?

Naturally, most people are still fascinated by the topic of personal survival. But only a negligible few want to know how their late Aunt Edith is making out, or whether Oscar Wilde's taken up screenwriting. Typically, they do not ask personal questions, but objective and practical ones: If we rack up bad karma, how long in the Penalty Box? What are the ground rules over there? And, increasingly, how can we best prepare for the Next Step *before* we die?

In this context, *Letters From Janice* at first seems to be something of a throwback. Like a bereaved sitter of the Victorian Era, Wayne Hatford is at first motivated by grief, wanting to re-establish contact with a long-time friend who has just departed physical existence. But Janice's replies are not comforting platitudes. Rather than write a posthumous "Dateline: Heaven" book like Bert Payson Terhune's *Across the Line,* she wastes no time in getting down to the multi-dimensional nitty-gritty, explaining not only what she's experiencing now, but what she wishes she'd understood while still "alive" in physical terms.

Quite inadvertently, *Letters From Janice* illustrates a principle that would-be channelers should keep in mind: The very best material comes through mediums who polish their verbal skills. Jane Roberts, for example, had been publishing poems, short stories, and novellas long before she made contact with Seth. Mr. Hatford teaches French and Spanish in Brookline, Massachusetts, schools and his English vocabulary, cross-pollinated with these Romance languages, is rich and flexible enough to give Janice room to express herself.

Readers who have sampled other classic channeled works like *The Unobstructed Universe* and *The Afterdeath Journal of an American Philosopher* will recognize a number of other familiar characteristics. For one thing, as Janice's letters continue, we sense an increasing gap between chronological Earth time and the "real" time through which Janice swims and cavorts. "There are no time constraints here," she writes. For another, she keeps remembering basic universal principles such as the Law of Inherent Rightness and the Law of Cause and

Effect, which we incarnates evidently seem to forget as soon as we enter the body at birth.

But perhaps most importantly, Janice displays what is practically a diagnostic trait among the newly-discarnate, and which resembles an earthly syndrome I recall from my Senior year in boarding school.

On very rare occasions, members of the previous year's graduating class would come back to visit. We undergraduates were really puzzled: Why did they return so seldom and so briefly to the campus that had been their entire world? Trying to talk with them, we could feel the emotional distance—and the implicit rebuff. They even seemed to stare *through,* not *at,* the very football field where they'd achieved an undefeated season.

Clearly, boarding school was still familiar to them; equally clearly, it no longer captured their interest at all. How, we wondered, could their formative years have paled for them so quickly—unless college was thoroughly and utterly different from anything we undergraduates could imagine?

Similarly, the "graduated" Janice displays a feeling of calm objectivity toward her life-just-past. Like many of the entities communicating today, she seems to have put behind her what Dante called "the dusty little threshing ground of Earth." Without a qualm, she recalls her poor physical health and fairly short lifespan and sees these apparent handicaps as basic, necessary tools she needed to achieve an overall balance.

Ironically, this almost scientific detachment among the newly-dead is precisely what frustrates ESP researchers seeking evidential proofs of life after death. Again and again, departed entities make only passing reference to their previous earthly existence, obviously because their focus is elsewhere. (Midterms and Spring Break are coming up, and who the hell *cares* who wrote what in the high school yearbook?)

This emotional distance also shapes the tone and flavor of most channeled messages. Communications that occur very soon after transition (like Janice's first replies) are most likely to be familiar and recognizable. But as Earth-time passes, the entity's attention continues to recede until what it communicates often becomes oddly condensed or abbreviated—full of loving emotions, perhaps, but disappointingly short on specifics.

Happily, Janice does not "fade" and remains a coherent presence. But even so, the reader can sense that she is beginning to evolve at an ever more rapid pace; and sometimes finds it impossible to report the full scope of those changes. With each new installment, she has quietly expanded a bit further into her Larger Self and sadly but inevitably, relays a bit less of what we can recognize as a time-bound, earthly personality.

But of course, that very alienation, that progressive distancing, is a vital part of her message! If Earth's graduates all remained in plain sight, this cramped three-dimensional nest might seem so cozy that we'd never want to leave. Sometimes, it takes the threat of loneliness and dissatisfaction to force us into trying our wings.

Letters From Janice, then, serves as a brisk primer for what each of us can expect in the next stage of our personal evolution. In addition, Janice provides a handy checklist of how best to pack for the journey: "Love is, again, the attitude to have prior to death. [It] helps you start the coming integration process. . . ." But best of all, this book is overwhelmingly comprehensible and, therefore, *reassuring*. "The Astral is the most fun you'll ever have," Janice avers, and she presents our afterdeath chores as such agreeable challenges that the worrisome concepts of fear and failure simply don't fit into the satchel.

On March 3, 1985, Janice's essential message comes through loud and clear: "Death requires a profound respect and a spirit of hopeful adventure. It provokes wonderment, joy, and rapture. It is hard to put these feelings into words." And yet she has done so, and so very well that anyone who peruses this book will be the richer for it.

Tam Mossman
Charlottesville, Virginia
Christmas, 1986

Wayne Hatford is a very clear channel who has done a fine job with the communications in this book. This is the time for many such channelings around the world. We at Uni-Sun have been privileged to publish several other excellent instances of books that have a high spiritual message. The global spiritual awakening has already begun and it is our intent to do all we can to add to its momentum. For a free copy of our catalog, write to:

Uni★Sun
P.O. Box 25421
Kansas City, Mo 64119
U.S.A.